Grow It Yourself!

Grow Your Own
Smoothie

John Malam

Raintree

www.raintreepublishers.co.uk
Visit our website to find out more information about Raintree books.

To order:
☎ Phone 0845 6044371
🖹 Fax +44 (0) 1865 312263
🖥 Email myorders@raintreepublishers.co.uk

Customers from outside the UK please telephone +44 1865 312262

Raintree is an imprint of Capstone Global Library Limited, a company incorporated in England and Wales having its registered office at 7 Pilgrim Street, London, EC4V 6LB – Registered company number: 6695582

Text © Capstone Global Library Limited 2012
First published in hardback in 2012
The moral rights of the proprietor have been asserted.

Edited by Daniel Nunn, Rebecca Rissman, and Sian Smith
Designed by Philippa Jenkins
Picture research by Mica Brancic
Production by Victoria Fitzgerald
Originated by Capstone Global Library Ltd
Printed and bound in China by Leo Paper Products Ltd

ISBN 978 1 406 22481 8
15 14 13 12 11
10 9 8 7 6 5 4 3 2 1

British Library Cataloguing in Publication Data
Malam, John, 1957-
  Grow your own smoothie. -- (Grow it yourself!)
  1. Fruit-culture--Juvenile literature. 2. Smoothies (Beverages)--Juvenile literature.
  I. Title II. Series
  634-dc22

Acknowledgements
The author and publisher are grateful to the following for permission to reproduce copyright material: Alamy pp. 9 (© Tetra Images), 15 (FoodPhotography Eising/© Bon Appetit), 21 (© Malcolm McMillan); © Capstone Publishers pp. 24. 25. 26, 27 (Karon Dubke); GAP Photos p. 29 (Dave Bevan); iStockphoto pp. 13 (© Alexander Raths), 14 (© Natalia Siverina), 17 (© johnnyscriv), 18 (© Viktor Kitaykin), 19 (© Chepko Danil), 22 (© Innershadows); Photolibrary pp. 6 (Garden Picture Library/Richard Clark), 7, 10 (Garden Picture Library/Andrea Jones), 11 (Animals Animals/Phil Degginger), 12 (Cultura/Adie Bush), 18 (Garden Picture Library/Sarah Cuttle); Shutterstock pp. 4 (© DenisNata), 5 (© Loskutnikov), 8 (© norr), 16 (© Elena Leonova), 20 (© Margarita Borodina), 23 (© Peter Elvidge).

Background cover photograph of strawberry fruit reproduced with permission of Shutterstock (© sydeen). Foreground cover photograph of a strawberry smoothie reproduced with permission of © Capstone Global Library Ltd (Philippa Jenkins).

Every effort has been made to contact copyright holders of material reproduced in this book. Any omissions will be rectified in subsequent printings if notice is given to the publisher.

To find out about the author, visit his website: www.johnmalam.co.uk

Some words are shown in bold, **like this**. You can find out what they mean by looking in the glossary.

Contents

Safety note:
Ask an adult to help you with
the activities in this book.

What is a strawberry?

A strawberry is the **fruit** of the strawberry plant. It is a soft fruit. It starts off green, then changes colour to red. When the **berry** is bright red, it is **ripe** and ready to pick.

This strawberry is ready to eat.

Strawberries grow close to the ground.

Strawberry plants make lots of tasty strawberries in the summer. Strawberries are good to eat, and can be used in many different ways.

Where to grow strawberries

Strawberry plants will grow in most types of garden soil. However, they don't like soil that gets very wet. They also don't like to be in the **shade**. They prefer to be in a sunny part of the garden.

This looks like a good place for strawberries to grow.

Pots for strawberries have holes in the side which the plants grow through.

Strawberry plants grow outside. They grow in the ground, but they can also be grown in large plant pots.

Prepare the ground

Start to get ready for growing strawberries in March or April. If you are going to grow them in the ground, you need to get the soil ready for the plants.

Clear the ground before planting the strawberry plants.

Compost is good for the soil.

Dig the soil with a gardening fork. Remove all the weeds. Add some **compost** to the soil. The compost will feed the strawberry plants and improve the soil.

9

Get ready to grow!

Start your strawberry patch off with baby plants. This is much quicker and easier than growing the plants from **seed**.

Baby strawberry plants are sold in trays. ▶

In April, buy some baby strawberry plants at a garden centre. Or, you could ask a gardener to let you have a few spare plants from their strawberry patch.

Planting and spacing

April and May are good months for strawberry plants to go into the ground. Dig a **shallow** hole where you want a strawberry plant to grow.

This plant is ready to go into the ground. ▶

Put one plant into the hole, then cover its **roots** with soil. Put more plants into the ground. Space them about 45 centimetres apart. Give them a drink of water.

When to water

Keep the plants watered, especially if it hasn't rained for a few days. If the plants are in pots, keep the soil **moist**. If the soil dries out, the plants will start to **wilt**.

This plant has not had enough water. It has wilted.

Use a watering can with a sprinkler.

When the plants start to make strawberries, be careful not to splash water on to them. If the **berries** get too wet, they might start to **rot**.

Don't forget the weeding!

Strawberries are low-growing plants. Weeds can easily cover them up. It's important to remove weeds before they take over the strawberry patch.

Keep the soil around the plants free from weeds. ▶

Remove as many weeds as you can.

Pull out larger weeds by hand, or dig them up with a **hand fork**. Be careful not to damage the strawberry plants.

Flowers and bees

In June and July, flowers appear on the plants. They have white petals and yellow centres. The flowers make yellow **pollen**.

white petals

yellow pollen

Strawberry plants make lots of flowers.

This bee will take pollen to another strawberry flower.

Bees come to the flowers. Pollen sticks to them. The bees move the pollen from one flower to another. After this, the plants start to make strawberries.

19

Caring for the plants

At first, the strawberries are small and green. As they grow, they will need protecting from slugs and birds.

Straw will keep the strawberries off the soil.

Garden netting will keep the birds away.

Put straw under the **berries**. It helps to keep slugs away, and keeps the strawberries clean. Cover the plants with garden **netting**. This stops birds from pecking at the juicy strawberries.

Here come the strawberries!

It only takes a few days for the green **berries** to grow to full-sized strawberries. Then they start to turn red.

Check the strawberries every day to see which ones are ripe.

Each plant will make lots of strawberries.

When the strawberries are red all over, they are **ripe** and ready to pick. Carefully pull them off the plant, one at a time. Try not to squash them!

Make a strawberry smoothie

You can turn your strawberries into a **fruit** drink called a **smoothie**. It has a lovely sweet taste. Ask an adult to help you with the cutting and blending.

You will need:
150 millilitres of natural yogurt,
300 millilitres of orange juice,
1 teaspoon of vanilla extract,
1 tablespoon of clear honey,
250 grams of strawberries,
1 banana, and
a blender.

1. Remove the stalks from the strawberries.
2. Cut the strawberries into pieces and slice the banana.
3. Put the chopped strawberries and banana into a blender.
4. Add the yogurt, vanilla extract, and clear honey.

4. Blend in the blender until the mixture is smooth.
5. Gradually add the orange juice. Blend until the juice is mixed in.

6. Pour into a jug. Place in a fridge until chilled.

7. Pour into tall glasses.
Drink through straws.

Get ready for next year

In August, the strawberry plants will make **runners**. These are long, thin shoots which run across the ground. At the ends of the runners are baby strawberry plants.

These runners have been pushed into small pots.

runner

When the plants have roots, ask an adult to cut the runners.

Carefully push the baby plants into the ground or a pot. In a few weeks they will have made **roots**. Ask an adult to cut the runners, so the babies are no longer joined to their parents. You now have new strawberry plants growing for next year!

Glossary

berry a juicy fruit that does not have a stone in the middle

compost loose, earthy material used for growing seeds and plants

fruit the part of a plant which can often be eaten as food. Fruit contains seeds.

hand fork a small gardening tool with three pointed prongs

moist when soil is damp but not too wet

netting a plastic net with holes in it

pollen tiny powdery grains made by flowers

ripe fully grown and ready to pick or eat

root the part of a plant that holds it in the ground. Roots collect water for the plant.

rot when fruit starts to go bad or mouldy

runners long, thin shoots from which new strawberry plants grow

seed the part of a plant that grows into a new plant

shade a darker area of the garden, where trees or buildings cast shadows

shallow not deep

smoothie a drink made from fresh fruit

wilt when a plant droops if it is thirsty

Find out more

Books to read

Grow It, Eat It, D. K. Publishing (Dorling Kindersley, 2008)

Ready, Steady, Grow!, Royal Horticultural Society (Dorling Kindersley, 2010)

Strawberries (Grow Your Own), Helen Lanz (Franklin Watts, 2010)

Websites

www.bbc.co.uk/gardening/basics/techniques/growfruitandveg_strawberries1.shtml
Find step-by-step instructions for growing strawberries on this website.

www.kiddiegardens.com
This site willl give you lots of ideas on how to grow plants that you can use to make things.

www.thekidsgarden.co.uk
Discover more gardening ideas and activities on this website.

Index